The Death Row Granny

Life of Serial Killer Velma Barfield

Jack Smith

All rights reserved. © 2024 by Jack Smith and Maplewood Publishing. No part of this publication or the information in it may be quoted from or reproduced in any form by means such as printing, scanning, photocopying, or otherwise without prior written permission of the copyright holder.

Efforts have been made to ensure that the information in this book is accurate and complete. However, the author and the publisher do not warrant the accuracy of the information, text, and graphics contained within the book due to the rapidly changing nature of science, research, known and unknown facts, and the internet. The author and the publisher do not hold any responsibility for errors, omissions, or contrary interpretation of the subject matter herein. This book is presented solely for motivational and informational purposes only.

Warning
Throughout the book, there are some descriptions of murders and crime scenes that some people might find disturbing. There might be also some language used by people involved in the murders that may not be appropriate.

Note
Words in italic are quoted words from verbatim and have been reproduced as is, including any grammatical errors and misspelled words.

ISBN 9798329596038

Printed in the United States

Contents

A Toxic Upbringing	1
Building A World of Deception	5
Velma Starts a Family	9
A Pattern of Passive Aggression Emerges	15
Moving on a Little Too Soon?	23
The Fixer	27
Velma Blues	31
Stage Managed Tragedy Continues to Strike	37
Sobering Realization	43
They Just Keep Dropping Like Flies	51
The Final Victim	57
Trial and Sentencing	65
It was Just an Accident	77
The Jury Has Decided	83
Further Readings	85

A Toxic Upbringing

There is an impression one gets of stark bleakness when looking out at the flatlands that make up the North Carolinian landscape where Velma Barfield grew up. Velma was born in her family's quaint home in Eastover, North Carolina, on October 29th, 1932. This newborn was the child of Murphy and Lillian Bullard.

There were no doctors or nurses in attendance, but her mother Lillian had the help of her husband Murphy, along with Murphy's mother and sister. With their efforts, little Margie Velma (later just dropped to Velma) was brought into this world.

She was born into a home that consisted of an extended family. Her dad Murphy had actually inherited the property from his elderly parents on the condition that he would look after them in their old age, as well as his disabled sister. His sister had suffered from a bout with polio that had left her paralyzed on one side.

Murphy, for his part, was a hard worker. He labored away at the local sawmill, often for lengthy shifts that seemed to stretch from early morning to late at night. He also took care of the family farm, growing food staples that would be crucial during the lean months. These were the days of the Great Depression after all, when most families were struggling just to get by.

Despite all of his efforts however, Murphy and his family members often just barely seemed to keep their heads above water. Murphy's dad in the meantime, had taken a turn for the worse, and passed away on February 5th, 1936 at 74 years of age. Murphy's mother also passed less than a year later.

While no one is accusing the toddler Velma with poisoning her own grandparents, the details of their passing are a bit jarring, considering what happened in Velma's later life. For the oddity of one person passing, only to be followed in short succession by their spouse, would indeed be a repeating pattern in Velma's later life and crimes.

Velma was only four years old at the time of her grandparents' passing however, and it's said that she had no conscious recollection of either of them in later life. The void of these passed elders, in the meantime would be filled by Velma's many siblings who were born in rapid succession. Velma had plenty of playmates, and her childhood should have been one full of joy and fun.

But as she grew older, her father's frustration with life grew deeper. And although he was known as a kind, considerate, hard-working man around town, at home he became a monster. The slightest disturbance was known to set him off—and violently so. Considering the fact that the man was overworked, and typically running on the fumes of a few hours of sleep, and perhaps the sudden caffeine boost in a cup of coffee—his penchant for having outbursts isn't all that surprising.

The violent nature of some of his outbursts however, are rather striking. He was especially known to take his anger out on his dogs. He had several hunting dogs, and if one of them somehow annoyed him, he didn't hesitate to kick, punch, and even stomp on the animals. On occasion, it's said he also struck them with a steel chain.

He reserved his leather belt in the meantime, for his own children. It might not have been quite as damaging as a steel chain, but it still felt bad enough to Velma and her siblings. She later recalled times in which she and her siblings were lined up and struck one by one, as if they were standing on their father's disciplinary assembly line.

The fact that one might be punished, whether they deserved it or not, by the authority figure of a parent, tends to make one despise authority itself. It seems that these sorts of feelings were likely inoculated within Velma from a young age, due to the wrath she had sustained at the hands of her father.

Despite her father's willingness to punish for even the slightest of perceived infractions, it's said that Velma was more resistant than the others. Even when threatened with more whippings, she was known to protest and talk back. A feat which caused Murphy to declare that she had a "smart mouth."

Along with fearing and despising her father Murphy, Velma came to greatly resent her mother Lillian, since in her view, her mom did absolutely nothing to defend her. The home is supposed to be a place of nourishment and support, not one of chaos, paranoia, and bitterness. Yet, this was indeed the classic brew of toxins in which the young Velma lived and grew up.

Building A World of Deception

Since she was a child, Velma had been seeking an exit. Almost from the start, it seems that she wished to exit right out of her family's poor, oppressed, and abusive household. She just didn't quite know how to do it. Her situation would improve ever so slightly in 1939 at the age of seven. For this was the year that she was able to finally go to school.

She was a first grader down at the old schoolhouse known simply as South River School. It wasn't much to look at, but the old brick building became a kind of refuge for Velma, since it allowed her to leave her troubled family home, at least on a temporary basis, throughout the week.

Velma, in fact wished she could stay at school all day, and wouldn't have minded one bit if her schooling continued into the summer. While other youngsters were happy when summer vacation arrived, Velma dreaded it. Velma was using school as her safe place of refuge.

All of this time spent at school, had the additional benefit of turning Velma into an ideal student. Ideal except for her occasional emotional outbursts. It seems that Velma, as much as she despised her father, had picked up some of his habits. Like him, the slightest thing could set her off.

This was especially the case if she felt that another student was trying to slight her in some fashion. Velma didn't hesitate to let the supposed offending student know how she felt. Her father had labeled her as having a "smart mouth" and Velma seemed to live up to this distinction at school by way of all of the smart-alecky comments that she made.

Some of her aggression against others apparently also stemmed from deep-rooted resentment. She was poorer than most of her other classmates, and this was evident in the worn-out old clothing that she wore. It bothered her to see other students with new shoes and outfits every year, while she was wearing the same old rags.

Velma was not only jealous of her classmates' better wardrobe, but also their better food. Velma's old schoolhouse seemed to lack a proper cafeteria, and all students were obligated to bring their lunch from home at her school. But some seemed to have better bag lunches than others.

While many other students had delicious-looking sandwiches on sliced bread, along with cookies and other special snacks bought from the local store, Velma would pull out a big hunk of day-old cornbread, accompanied by a nasty-looking piece of shriveled up sausage.

Some of her peers were merciless in their taunts, and took to even making fun of these morsels that Velma gnawed on at lunch. She was so bothered by their remarks, she often took her bag of lunch out in the woods and ate by herself, just to avoid their jeers. It was her resentment over her classmates' better repasts in the meantime, that inspired her first steps into a life of crime.

She began to actually steal money right out of her father's pants pockets. This was quite a feat, considering the fear he supposedly generated. She apparently overcome her fear enough to rob him of small amounts of money. Cash which she used it to buy herself snacks from the local store.

Velma always did like her snacks. It was a lifelong craving she maintained until her dying day when she was executed by way of lethal injection. Her last meal after all, consisted of a bag of cheez doodles (if it's good for Chester Cheetah who are we to judge?) and a can of Coca-Cola.

So, after stealing money from her old man and using the ill-gotten proceeds to buy her fill of snacks from the local store, she would sit down right in front of her judgmental classmates and munch on chips, candy, and moon pies to her heart's delight.

Papa Murphy however, eventually did catch wind of his daughter's petty thefts—not from his own pocket—but from someone else's. For a man who lived nearby came to him complaining that $80 had gone missing from his home, right after Velma was seen wandering around his property. She was found with the money, and her father promptly gave her a whipping.

In the middle of the beating, she tried to use that "smart mouth" of hers and made up a story that the man had asked her to hold the cash for him. Her defense was basically—"Yeah! I have his money, but I didn't steal it, I was just holding it for him." This childish explanation was absurd to anyone who heard it, but this was Velma's first real attempt to obscure the facts when she was found doing something very wrong. It was the beginning of a habit of deception that she would continue to rely upon.

A habit which would come to the surface one final time during her trial in later life when she insisted to an incredulous prosecutor that *yes, she killed people, but she didn't do it on purpose, it was an accident.* Without blinking an eye, she would insist that she just wanted to make people sick, and the fact that several of those she tried to make ill died, was nothing more than the merest of accidents.

The jury wouldn't be persuaded by this bogus argument any more than Papa Murphy was persuaded by Velma's deception as a child. Determined to get to the bottom of what Velma was up to, Murphy embarked upon his own impromptu inquisition. It took some effort—and likely more than a few hits from his belt—but eventually Velma admitted to what she had done. Any future admissions to the mistakes and outright crimes that she committed would not be quite so forthcoming.

Velma Starts a Family

If you hear her tell it—Velma described her childhood home life as nothing but hardship, drudgery, and pain. But of course, most psychopathic killers do tend to make their own childhood sound as terrible as possible, in order to elicit as much sympathy as they possibly can. With that in mind, we would be wise to take her recollections with a grain of salt.

Even Velma in fact, had to admit that it wasn't *all* bad—she could remember some bright spots of her youth, and even a few kind moments from her old Papa Murphy. Murphy, it seems was a huge baseball fan, and would encourage the whole family to partake in an ad hoc game of baseball on Sunday afternoons. Sunday was apparently the day he had off, and he used it to slightly relent on his harsh rule and allow for a little bit of fun.

According to Velma it was as if he was a whole "other person" during these baseball games. Instead of being a mean, belligerent bully, he was happy, playful, and kind. Velma herself enjoyed these outings, and later recalled with relish how she played the position of shortstop, tasked with making sure the ball got to base on time so the defending team could tag the runner out. They all apparently enjoyed the baseball games a great deal, as evidenced by the fact that the games would often last until the sun went down.

Velma in her youth was a rough and tumble child, and she enjoyed baseball as much as pure and simple roughhousing. It was in the 4th grade however, that her penchant for rambunctiousness would get her in trouble. She was running across the playground at school when she slammed head-first into another student. She apparently didn't see the boy, but he seemed to have the stronger head of the two.

For even though he shook off the collision, she fell down and was knocked out. When she came to, she had a large, painful bump on her head. The bump never completely went away, and even though it was only slightly visible in later years, she would be painfully aware of it. This slight blemish on her forehead would inspire many of her later hairdos. Yes indeed, for some acne-scarred and pockmarked men, a beard might cover a multitude of sins; but for Velma, it was stylish hair bangs that would do the trick.

Nevertheless, as she grew older, she had increasing feelings of inadequacy about her appearance, it was actually her father who seemed to help her self-esteem during this period. She can recall that by the time she entered adolescence, her dad treated her much more gently. In one of the few loving memories she had of Murphy, she later recollected how he began to call her, "Honey" and "Sugar."

As a young teen, he even surprised Velma on one occasion, by buying her a nice dress she had been interested in wearing. She would wear that dress with pride, hoping that the stylish threads would lift her up out of her drab existence. If she was looking for extra attention at this age, her wish to be noticed was soon fulfilled, for it was when she was in her early teens, that the boys began calling.

One boy in particular, a certain Thomas Burke began to call in a bit too much, as far as Velma's father was concerned. So much so, that he forbade her to see him, and insisted that she not even *think* about dating until she turned 16. At first Velma abided by her father's wishes, but even after she turned 16, her father still tried to shelter her from boys. Velma decided to ignore his instructions.

She began to see Thomas, first at church functions, then among mutual groups of friends. Despite her father's dislike of the boy, soon enough, Thomas was coming to pick Velma right up from her home. She must have viewed Thomas as the clear vehicle through which she could exit her unhappy home life for good. Soon Thomas and Velma were spending a lot of time together.

One of their favorite haunts was the local drive-in. Here a teenager with a car, and some money for the latest feature, could take their sweetheart to a secure spot, where they wouldn't be bothered by pesky family members trying to interfere. Even so, Velma knew that she had to get home, eventually. Her father had set a strict curfew and she was to be home by 10pm. She didn't dare miss this deadline, no matter how good the movie—*or Thomas' company*—might have been.

If she were late, her father might not hit her with a belt—she was finally deemed too old for that—but he would lecture her for hours. Even worse, he would put severe restrictions on any future outings. In Velma's mind, cutting a make-out session short, was much preferable to being grounded for the foreseeable future. Nevertheless, Velma did manage to incur just this sort of wrath during her relationship with Thomas.

Teenage Velma had been sick of her family telling her what to do, and had actually decided that she was going to leave home, for good. She had apparently made arrangements to stay with her brother's fiancée. Feeling that she had a secure place to run off to, she left a note for her parents, stating that she no longer wanted to live under their roof, and simply left.

As soon as Murphy found out, he was furious, and had his wife Lillian join him, to track their wayward daughter down. Demonstrating how much of a pull of authority the man had, after he got through screaming and yelling, he was able to successfully get Velma into his car. After getting back home, Murphy didn't resort to the belt—*but Lillian did.*

It was after her mother had given the girl a whipping that Murphy told Velma that she was grounded, and not allowed to see Thomas any more. Thomas was a senior in high school at the time, and Velma feared losing him after he graduated. As such, she secretly saw him whenever she could, in the hopes of keeping their relationship alive. Fortunately for Velma, after she turned 17, her dad had a change of heart, and gave his consent for her to see the boy again.

Murphy, in his heart of hearts, must have realized that these two really did care for each other. However, when the couple decided to take matters into their own hands and run off and get married, Murphy was ready for all-out war. It was apparently Thomas' idea for them to cross state lines and elope in a jurisdiction that didn't require parental consent (Velma was still only 17).

After Murphy figured out what had happened, he blew up on just about everyone within reach and demanded that the marriage be annulled. Ultimately however, he had lost control of his daughter. She was now on her own and was living life on her own terms. Both she and her new husband promptly dropped out of high school, got jobs to support themselves, and moved into their own home.

Thomas did many odd and temporary jobs. He worked on farms, in factories, and he drove a truck for a soda bottle company. Velma worked for a time at a local drugstore, until Thomas persuaded her to quit. These were the days after all, when many men were still uncomfortable with their wives working, and encouraged them to stay at home.

Thomas, despite his own inability to provide enough income, was very much of this mindset. He had decided that if dough was going to be earned for the household, he would be the one to earn it—end of story. He wanted her to stay home and take care of any kids they might have. The first of which came kicking and screaming into the world on December 15th, 1951, when Velma and Thomas' son, named Ronald (otherwise known as Ronnie), was born.

Velma loved her new baby boy, and in many ways, the non-judgmental affection she felt from the newborn stirred in her something that she had never felt before—*unconditional love*. She didn't have to do chores, follow instructions, or somehow perform for this baby. This child loved her no matter what she did.

Encouraged by the experience, Velma was soon pregnant again, and birthed a daughter on September 3rd, 1953. She named the little girl Pamela.

She was close with the kids, and remained so until they were old enough to start school. Parting from them however, proved difficult. When her son Ronnie started elementary school, Velma was one of those parents that had to remain with her clinging child during the first day, just to make sure that he wasn't too anxious.

Ronnie took to his schooling soon enough however, and so too did Pamela. This meant that whether she liked it or not, Velma suddenly had a lot of free time during the day. At first, she tried to make the most use of it by once again getting a job.

By the late 1950s, attitudes about women working away from home were finally beginning to change, and Thomas grudgingly allowed her to get a job. She ended up working at a local textile plant. She was sure to use the extra money she had to spoil her kids any way she could. For one thing was certain, she was determined to give them the happy childhood that she felt had been denied to her.

A Pattern of Passive Aggression Emerges

As the 1950s merged into the 1960s, things were looking up for Velma and her family. They were financially on better footing after Thomas received employment as a driver for Pepsi Cola. His paychecks increased, and soon he and his wife and kids were moving into a new, much more spacious house. The house was not only bigger, but so too was the accompanying yard.

The kids in particular, were thrilled to have a huge backyard to run around in. It was this same backdrop, which became the setting for countless backyard barbeques in which family and friends got together to relax and unwind. Velma would need the relaxation, for in 1963 she faced an unexpected health scare. She apparently woke up one day bleeding heavily from her vagina.

She was around 30 years old at the time, and had never experienced anything quite like this in the past. She immediately went to the doctor. Upon further examination, it was discovered that she had a bad case of fibroid tumors growing from her uterus. The doctor's insisted she would need a hysterectomy. For women who have not yet had children, such news is absolutely devastating.

Velma and Thomas, however, were quite happy with the two kids they had, so the decision to go forward with the procedure—although frightening—was still much easier for them to make, than it otherwise might have been. But there were certain after-effects that Velma had no idea that she would experience.

There was not a lot of education in those days on hormone imbalances, and what they can do to a person. Velma had no way of knowing that the hysterectomy would make her own hormone levels so off kilter that she might feel out of sorts. But according to those who knew her best, she seemed to be a changed woman after the procedure. She became much more anxious, and suffered through bouts of depression.

Even worse, she began to take her frustrations out on both her husband as well as her children. No one seemed to know just how to handle her wild mood swings, yet they just kept right on coming. Around this time, she also became conscious about her weight. She felt that she was steadily putting on the pounds and wanted to trim down a bit. These concerns led her to ask a doctor to prescribe some diet pills.

The pills might have helped her to lose a little weight, but they made her even more anxious and hyper. The effect of these pills would then be compounded by some pain pills prescribed a few years later. The pain pills were given for back pain she had been experiencing. Velma and her doctors thought they were treating legitimate conditions and concerns at the time, but they were also paving the way for addiction and subsequent increasingly unpredictable behavior on Velma's part.

As was evidenced, on one occasion in particular, when Velma took too many pills, got in her car, and blacked out. During this episode she went right off the road and through someone's yard, nearly hitting the side of a house. She claimed at the time to be entirely oblivious as to the reason for this accident. She insisted she had no idea how such a thing had happened. But everyone around her knew that she had been popping pills.

Rather than cut down however, she would soon be taking even *more* pills. It was in 1963 that the FDA approved Valium to the public, and soon this anti-anxiety drug would find its way to Velma's medicine cabinet.

Velma's marriage to Thomas, in the meantime, had been falling apart at the seams. It was a gradual dissolution at first, but like is so often the case, the distance between them quickly became vast, and the next thing they knew, they were something more like roommates than a married couple.

On the surface, things looked great. They had been married for 15 years, had a steady income, supportive friends, and two happy, well-adjusted kids. Yet cracks had appeared in their relationship. One point of contention was that Thomas had started hanging out with a local social club, and during club meetings, indulged in a drink or two. When Velma found out she was livid.

Thomas didn't think it was a big deal to drink every so often, but Velma equated drunkenness with her heavy-drinking father. And if Thomas so much as took a sip of alcohol, she felt as if he were transforming into the same kind of drunken tyrant.

Ironically, as her kids would later recall, the sheer hostility that Velma unleashed on her unsuspecting husband was the closest thing to tyranny that anyone had ever witnessed. She became unreasonable, and belligerent and ready to pick a fight. In other words—*Velma had become her father.*

Yes, it is indeed one of the greatest ironies of life, that in their efforts to stamp out something they dislike, folks often become the very thing they hate. This is apparently precisely what had happened with Velma Barfield. Their relationship was falling apart, and the unexpected death of Thomas Burke's father, John, put even more stress on their failing marriage. The home had become so volatile at this point, Velma's kids tried to stay away as much as possible.

Ironically enough, one of the best refuges they had was with their grandparents, Murphy and Lillian. Yes indeed, Murphy, who now presented himself as a kind and doting grandfather, was now considered much better to be around than Velma. Velma had become what she had hated, and was driving her own kids into the arms of her reformed father, Murphy, who was now considered a much more pleasant person than she was.

The arguments continued in the meantime, and Ronnie the oldest child often felt thrust into the position of peacemaker. It was really an impossible task, and the most he could do was minimize the damage. As was the case after one particularly explosive argument in which the quick-thinking Ronnie saved his father from a potentially nasty injury.

The two had been arguing all night before a drunk Thomas passed out on the couch.

Just prior to this, Thomas has dropped a bottle that had shattered on the floor. Velma, the ever-meticulous housewife, was sure to sweep the mess up, but in the process, she shoved the pile of broken glass right by the couch where her husband was sleeping. She positioned it perfectly enough so that as soon as he woke up and put his feet on the ground, he likely would have stepped on it, barefoot.

It might not seem like much, but he could have seriously hurt himself in the process. In fact, if the jagged, broken glass managed to slice through an artery, he could have possibly bled to death on the spot. This would have made Thomas suddenly Velma's murder victim Number One. Even though Velma would never own up to it.

After Ronnie dutifully moved the pile of swept glass safely away from his father, and he asked his mother what she was up to, she was quick to play dumb. He asked her why she did it, and she simply shrugged her shoulders and acted like she didn't know what he was talking about.

She could pretend all she wanted however, but her intent was clear. She put that broken glass there in the hopes that her husband would step on it and get injured. She simply wanted to orchestrate his injury in a passive-aggressive enough manner, so that she could later employ plausible deniability. What happened? How did Thomas get hurt? *I don't know! I was just trying to clean up some broken glass!*

This one passive-aggressive act of last-minute malice Velma executed at the end of a late-night argument, presents itself as a rather innocuous incident at first glance, but it's not. For this was the start of a pattern of passive-aggressive attacks that would eventually lead to outright murder.

As Velma continued popping pills and her husband Thomas dived even deeper into what was now full-blown alcoholism, a once loving marriage was falling apart. Matters became considerably worse in the meantime, when Thomas was pulled over and hit with a DUI charge. The judge gave him considerable slack by helping him avoid jail time. Thomas was ultimately given a suspended sentence, a suspended license, and a personal warning from the judge.

Even so, it was a devastating blow to Thomas' pride. He now couldn't even drive himself to work, and had to hitch a ride with friends and co-workers. Instead of straightening up his routine, he began to drink even *more* heavily than ever before. Velma still tried to provoke him into shouting matches in the meantime, but Thomas, apparently realizing he couldn't change her behavior, opted to change his own.

He no longer engaged with his wife when she threw her tantrums, he learned to simply ignore her. She could be screaming just a few inches from his face, and between taking sips from his beer, he simply stared straight ahead, as if he didn't hear her. Their two kids Ronnie and Pamela couldn't figure out what was worse: the terrible arguments of the past, or their dad's new tactic of despondent silence.

It was all just too much for anyone to bear. Worse was yet to come however, when Velma utilizing all of the conniving tools at her disposal, had her depressed, alcoholic husband forcibly committed. It's unclear what her motive may have been at the time. Perhaps she really was trying to help him—who's to say? But ultimately it had a disastrous affect.

After Thomas was released, he felt as if he had been made a marked man. In the small town they lived in, everyone knew everyone else's business, and now he felt that all of the townspeople were talking about him behind his back. As a result, he drew even further into his own shell, as he continued to try and drown his pain with alcohol.

Velma, in the meantime, turned out to be the one who really needed to be committed. For one fine day in 1967, she ended up having a nervous breakdown of sorts and was hospitalized. After she was suitably calmed down, the doctors prescribed her even more pills to pop.

More tragedy would occur in 1969 in the meantime, when Thomas was found dead from an apparent housefire. He had supposedly fallen asleep in one of his many drunken stupors with a cigarette in his hand. He was alone at the time, yet Velma had managed to mysteriously arrive right on the scene just before he perished. She was the one who called for help and brought emergency personnel to the scene.

Nevertheless, Thomas, who was only 38 years old, perished from smoke inhalation. It was deemed an accident at the time even though the circumstances were a bit suspicious. Yes, just like that pile of broken glass that Thomas once almost "accidentally" stepped on, his demise was deemed accidental. Nothing more and nothing less.

But several years after the fact, folks wouldn't be quite so sure.

Moving on a Little Too Soon?

Velma's son Ronnie was all for his mother being able to move on from his father's passing, and try to have some sort of happiness in life, but when she suddenly announced she was getting married, he could hardly believe it. She gave him and his sister the shocking news in 1970, scarcely a year after their father had died. Ronnie, typically, tried to be supportive.

He knew the elder widower Jennings Barfield, that Velma had her sights on, and he knew that he was a good man. Ronnie mused that perhaps the marriage would help stabilize Velma, and encourage her to kick her drug habit. Pamela however, strongly disagreed. First of all, she was outraged that her mother was moving on so quickly from her father.

Such feelings are perhaps natural for many children to feel, when their widowed parent declares that they are going to remarry. But secondary to this feeling that her mother was betraying her father's memory, Pamela actually voiced concerns for Mr. Barfield.

It wasn't that she thought he would be bad for her mother, she fully agreed with Ronnie that Jennings Barfield was a good man. She was in fact worried about *what her mother might put this poor man through*, should they get married. Although Ronnie had a much more charitable view of his mother and her struggles, Pamela did not.

She made no such excuses for her mother's substance abuse, and she also more readily recalled how she had treated her late father. Pamela essentially took one look at Jennings Barfield, the kindly older gentleman, and feared for his safety! She went so far as to arrange a secret meeting with Barfield at her grandpa Murphy's home.

Here they sat on the porch and made small talk, until Pamela got to the point. She told Jennings that she felt that her mother wasn't right for him. In fact, she stressed that her mother might be *very bad for him*. Barfield however, seemed to slough it all off as the jitters of a child not ready for a blended family. He essentially assured her that everything would be fine, before patting her on the hand and bidding her farewell.

That was the last chance that Pamela had to give the old man forewarning. But her bid to scare him off (apparently for his own good!) didn't seem to work. And the two got hitched and became Mr. and Mrs. Barfield on August 23rd, 1970 regardless. Velma immediately moved in with the 54-year-old Jennings and his 16-year-old daughter who still lived at home at that time.

The old family home of Velma and her children had been undergoing remodeling ever since the fire, and Pamela and Ronnie had essentially moved in with their grandparents. It was an odd sort of arrangement that was likely to provoke a lot of bitterness.

One can only imagine what it must feel like to have their father perish, only for their mother to run off, get married, and move in with another man a year later, leaving her children to practically fend for themselves.

There was a bright spot in all of this for Ronnie however, since Velma informed him that she had convinced the well-to-do Jennings to pay for his first semester of college. Ronnie had since graduated high school and had held out hope that he could gain a secondary education. He was happy to find out that the University of South Carolina would indeed accept him, as long as his new stepdad Jennings paid for the first semester as promised.

Ronnie arrived on campus ready to live in the dorm, only to be told that his tuition had not been paid. He checked back home, only to find that Jennings was clueless about the arrangement. He had never agreed to pay his tuition. Ronnie could only assume that there had been some sort of misunderstanding. But the more he thought about the bizarre situation that both he and Jennings had found themselves in, he couldn't help but wonder.

He couldn't help but wonder if his mother had tried to engineer the whole situation, so that Jennings would feel obliged to pay something he never agreed to in the first place. Perhaps Velma felt that she could orchestrate payment of Ronnie's tuition through manipulation and deceit, but Jennings ultimately just wasn't going to have it.

Even so, upon speaking with his mother, she continued to insist that he stay at university and they would find a way to pay. After continually checking with the university's financial aid office only to be embarrassed and reminded that he had no means to pay, Ronnie had to face up to facts. He had to accept both that he had no way to pay for his education, and that his mother had somehow completely disconnected herself from reality.

He realized study wasn't happening, and considering that the Vietnam war was raging and ready to draft him at any time, he decided to beat them to the punch. Instead of going to university, he joined up with the military. For him, it was his only ticket away from the depths of chaos that his own mother had descended into.

But even this would not quite work out as planned, because right before his date to ship out neared, fate (or perhaps better put; the conniving way of his mother) intervened once again. In 1971, he received a frantic call from Velma, with her shouting that Jennings Barfield had died.

The old man's heart had simply given out. Ronnie was amazed at the terrible luck his mother seemed to be having, and agreed to rush right over to her side. But soon enough, it would be learned that luck had nothing to do with the men who were falling dead at Velma Barfield's feet.

The Fixer

It's hard to believe that someone would be conniving enough to kill their husband just to stop their eldest son from shipping off to a life in the military. But in consideration of what transpired in the life of Velma and her children, this seems to be at least part of her motivation for the deed. For it was through the death of Jennings and her own put-on show of grief, that she managed to emotionally blackmail Ronnie into reconsidering his deployment.

But little did Velma know, she was now up against an opponent who was far more determined than even she was. For even though Ronnie, at the behest of his mother's needling, petitioned the army to let him out of his military duties in light of all of her suffering, the U.S. Army flat out refused.

Ronnie was shipping out to basic training—end of story.

Velma would bitterly complain about how uncaring the U.S. government was (not for Ronnie—but for her!) for the rest of her days. Nevertheless, she couldn't win with Uncle Sam and despite all of her attempts to manipulate events from behind the scenes, Ronnie ended up at basic training in Fort Jackson, South Carolina, just as planned.

Even so, his mother continued to demand that he press his superior officers for a "hardship discharge." The most recent disturbance was an apparent break-in. Ronnie however, would later learn that his mother had staged the incident—just like she had staged so many other things in her life.

Nevertheless, as she continued to have "problems" he continued to haggle with his superior officers. As testament to the recent "troubles" that they had been having, he collected both the death certificates of his father Thomas, as well as his stepfather—however briefly he had played the role, Jennings Barfield.

He also collected the endless letters from his mother's doctors which highlighted her various "nervous conditions." Velma in the meantime, had been staying with her own mother and father. As much as she later claimed to have been "afraid" of her Papa Murphy and to "resent" her mother Lillian, it's pretty strange how even as a middle-aged woman, she ended up living under their roof and utilizing their resources, completely free of charge,, of course.

As much as she later condemned her parents, at this stage, it was clearly the latter who were suffering— *suffering from Velma.* Her father Murphy in particular, seemed to have strange and chronic health ailments and they strangely coincided with the times that Velma was staying under his roof. He got so sick at one point in fact, he had to take time off work, in order to recover. The more he was home however, the worse he seemed to get.

Velma was still having her own episodes in the meantime. Her poor frazzled mother Lillian was beside herself on how to deal with her grown up daughter. She often found Velma unresponsive in bed, apparently due to an overdose from the pills she was popping. She had to call emergency services on occasion to have Velma taken to seek mental health care.

Here she spoke to counselors, and in one instance she gave a startling reason for taking too many pills. She told the therapist that she had attempted to end her life. The reason? She didn't want to see her son die in Vietnam. After getting over the (much intended) shock value of her words, one can see the selfish, self-serving nature of Velma's antics.

She was afraid her son would die in Vietnam—so she wanted to kill herself? Just so she wouldn't have to deal with his funeral? So, it was OK if he died as long as she didn't have to be bothered with funeral arrangements? Was that what she was trying to say? She couldn't stand the thought of living through all that—so she attempted suicide?

It really didn't make much sense, but the episode was all part of her pressure campaign to get her son discharged from the military so that he could "take care of her needs." She figured that if the doctors wrote up a good report about how Ronnie's deployment was driving her to suicide, perhaps then the U.S. military would finally listen and grant the request.

Ronnie for his part, dutifully forwarded the information to his superior officers, and although they weren't willing to grant a discharge, they were willing to solve that little problem about her supposed fears that he might die in Vietnam. They reassigned him to Fort Bragg, right in North Carolina.

Grandpa Murphy's health took a turn for the worse in the meantime, and the doctors gave him a bad report. He was dying of terminal lung cancer. He went into a swift decline after this, and perished on April 15th, 1973 at the age of 61. Velma meanwhile, added to her increasing irresponsibility by letting the house that her late husband Jennings had worked so hard on, go into foreclosure.

She had ceased making payments long ago, and the property finally reached the point of no return, and was seized by the state. In the aftermath, Velma was put back into a mental health facility. This time around, she made a friend during her stay, Al Smith, a 60-year-old construction worker who was being treated for alcoholism.

The pairing was bizarre on many levels. Velma was right around 40 years old at the time, and was getting involved with a man who was about the same age as her recently deceased father. Besides the age gap, the most glaring aspect of all this, was that she was spearing her hooks into a guy who was apparently afflicted with the same exact problem that she constantly belittled her late first husband Thomas for—*alcoholism.*

She had ranted and raved and repeatedly shoved poor Thomas' nose into the dirt over his alcohol addiction, yet now she was willfully cozying up with a guy who had the same exact condition. It's said that there are those who seek out broken people with a desire to "fix them." Perhaps this was the big draw for Velma. Unfortunately for her new flame Mr. Al Smith, Velma's method of "fixing" folks often left them feeling *much* worse for wear.

Velma Blues

Shortly after she got out of the clinic, Velma was back in her family home, living with her now-widowed mother, Lillian Bullard. Lillian must have been surprised when a short time later, she was joined by a man who was old enough to be her father—*Al Smith*. Mr. Smith had just gotten out of the clinic for alcohol addiction and had sworn that he was ready to get his life back on track.

Mr. Smith was a divorced father of two grown children, and had three grandkids he doted on. He now also had a new girlfriend 20 years younger than himself in the form of Velma. She seemed to be a lady truly interested in him, and most importantly interested in his recovery. Al Smith likely felt that he had lucked out in finding her. Unfortunately for him however, *his luck would soon run out.*

Velma's son Ronnie in the meantime, was deeply suspicious of the whole arrangement. He absolutely could not believe that his mother was hooking up with a guy who was afflicted with the same problem of alcoholism that she had condemned his late father for. Velma however, insisted that Al Smith was a man on the mend.

She also took him to church services with her, as if to prove to everyone that her man had been "fixed". Ronnie and others would remain skeptical, but Ronnie for his part felt that if it made his mom happy, he better just leave well alone.

Velma for her part, seemed to briefly improve. She got a steady job and (to Lillian's great relief) even managed to move out of her mother's house. She moved into her own apartment, a small unit above a garage, in Whiteville, South Carolina. It wasn't much, but it was at least a place to call her own.

As much as Ronnie tried to be happy for his mother however, she was nowhere near as charitable for him. Ronnie had been dating a local lady named Joanna for some time, and the two had become pretty serious. His mother was not at all happy, when Ronnie announced his intention to get married.

Velma outright exploded when she heard the news, and began to go into an emotional tirade about how he was going to get married and forget all about her. She even had the gall to berate her son for the expensive ring that he had bought his bride to be, declaring that all of the money spent toward it could have—*who would have guessed?*—come to her!

In Velma's self-centered narcissistic world, where all proceeds should be immediately deposited into her emotional—as well as financial—account, the fact that her son dared to meet a woman, and attempt to start a life of his own was perceived as a terrible affront. Ronnie tried to calm his mother down, and insisted that he would still have plenty of time with her even after he was married—but she was inconsolable.

So much so, that when Ronnie set his and Joanna's wedding date for later that February, his mom took the initiative to create such a ruckus that she was all but guaranteed to disrupt it. For before the year was out, she overdosed on pills so badly, she was in a coma and placed on a respirator. If it wasn't for immediate intervention in fact, she very well could have died.

It's a pretty sick person who would risk killing themselves just to get attention and manipulate all of the people in their lives, but this was indeed Velma's own unique style of calling card. She couldn't handle the attention suddenly shifting from herself to Joanna and Ronnie's wedding—and even if it meant nearly killing herself to get the spotlight back onto her narcissistic self, she was willing to do it.

She could not care less about the wracking guilt that her son Ronnie felt, as he stood by his comatose mother's bedside. He blamed himself for the whole thing of course, because if he had only *not* announced he was getting married, none of this would have happened. Or at least, that's what Velma wanted him to believe.

It was only after his mother recovered, that Ronnie began to reconsider what was happening to him. As she turned the corner and it became clear that she would indeed survive, he began to think things over quite a bit and he came to realize just how tired he was of his mother trying to control his life. As soon as she was up and talking, he had what amounted to a stern lecture with her, in which "the son" seemed to almost act like "the parent".

He told his mother that she needed to get her life back together but until she did, he suggested she go back to live with her own mother, Lillian. He also informed her that he was going to get married, and no matter what she did, she couldn't stop him. It seems that either Velma finally took her son at his word, or she had simply run out of steam as far as her own will to resist was concerned, but she seemed—if not to give her consent—to silently agree.

She even managed to participate in the wedding. She took part even though Ronnie had to hold his breath the entire time, fearing that she might somehow have another episode and ruin the whole thing. But to his relief, the wedding ceremony went forward without any problems or interruptions. He and Joanna were lawfully wedded, husband and wife.

They moved into an apartment together, and began to start their new life. Ronnie very much hoped his mother would be able to get her act together. His hope however, was dashed, when his mom randomly called him one fine evening from the county jail. She was being held on charges of forgery. She had apparently attempted to forge herself a new prescription of pills, by imitating a doctor's signature.

The keen eyes of the pharmacist determined that something was up however, and upon double-checking, figured out that the prescription had been forged. Police were notified and Velma was tossed into the slammer. Velma ended up pleading guilty to the charges, and received a suspended sentence, along with a $100 fine.

The judge was taking it easy on her, but was quick to advise her to straighten out her life, because the courts wouldn't be so merciful for another infraction of this kind.

Ronnie meanwhile, finally got his discharge from the military. This was the one bright spot for Velma during this period, since she now felt she could have her son back. It was with her son close at hand however, that Velma would be at her toxic worst.

Stage Managed Tragedy Continues to Strike

Ronnie felt like a new man after his release from the military. His wife had since gone to college at Pembroke State University, and Ronnie decided he would likewise follow suit. He had been denied college after the strange mix-up with Jennings Barfield, but now he thought he just might be able to take classes without interference. In the Fall of 1973, he arranged his courseload, so that he could work and go to university at the same time. He would be busy—but he would be fulfilled.

Not everything would work out as planned however, and soon there was strain on Ronnie's marriage. This bit of strain he could not blame on his mother, and after a shouting match with Joanna devolved into him taking a baseball bat to their telephone, Ronnie realized that he had some things he needed to work out as well. The couple managed to patch things up however, and soon Ronnie found an unexpected niche for himself.

He had begun playing golf on the side for fun, but after he proved to be surprisingly good at it, and was actually paid to participate in tournaments; his part-time hobby of golfing, turned into a full-time gig. The situation with his mother in the meantime, wasn't getting much better.

Velma was still staying with her own mom Lillian, and was barely able to hold a job. She seemed to switch employers every few months in fact. Even worse, she managed to get on the wrong side of the law once again. Despite the previous judge's warnings, she once again committed forgery. This time not for a fake prescription but for a fake check. This time around, for her efforts, she was given jail time.

She was made to stay in jail for 30 days, of a six-month suspended sentence. Yet, even *that* didn't teach her a lesson. For soon, Velma was at it once again. She began forging checks from her mother, in order to pay for her drug habit. Velma's mom Lillian knew that something was up when she began to notice money mysteriously leaving her accounts, but she didn't know how to confront Velma, and she didn't want to get the law involved.

Despite her problems, Velma was still her daughter after all, and she figured having her thrown behind bars wouldn't help anyone. This is of course, what many kind-hearted mothers of troubled adult children tend to think. But sadly enough, in Lillian's case, she likely would have been better off if she had turned her daughter in, and allowed the courts to throw the book at her. If she had done so, Lillian might have lived a little bit longer, at the very least.

Lillian's inaction only enabled Velma to get worse, and by 1974, she had once again hit rock bottom; she was unemployed and strung out on drugs on a daily basis. The relationship between Velma and her mother, in the meantime, had gone from bad to worse. Lillian was likely resentful that her middle-aged daughter was still living with her, and causing her all of these problems.

Part of that resentment might have come out when during Velma's few moments of clarity, Lillie tried to get her to do some chores. Velma however, apparently having flashbacks to when she was a kid and how much she hated household chores back then, wasn't having it. Ronnie walked in on one of these distressing instances in which Lillian had apparently triggered Velma.

Lillie had simply asked Velma to do some laundry, and Velma started screaming and throwing clothes all over the house. Not exactly a flattering image Ronnie got of his own mother, to see her acting like a four-year-old, throwing a tantrum and screaming at grandma Lillian—but this is apparently what happened. Velma now, just as when she was a child, highly resented anyone telling her what to do.

Since she was a full-grown woman that should have been living on her own and taking care of herself, her resentment was even further compounded by her frustration at not being able to stand on her own two feet. Or as Ronnie himself would later put it, "I think there was more anger in my mom then than I had ever seen. And it was a different type than I'd seen before, all directed at my grandmother. She just seemed to have a lot of resentment. She resented having to depend on her mother."

But she was broke and unemployed with nowhere else to go. It was her fault, yet she was ready to take out her wrath on her own mother Lillian, who was only trying to help her. Her trouble with money however, was soon eased a bit, when Velma's boyfriend Al Smith suddenly turned up dead. In August of 1974, he was run over by a truck, and as it just so happens, he had left money to Velma, since she had been made the beneficiary of his life insurance policy.

Considering the facts that came out towards the end of Velma's life, we shouldn't' hesitate to view such things through the lens of suspicion. For one thing, how did Velma end up the beneficiary of this guy's life insurance? She had only been dating him a short time. Did she pressure and cajole him into it? Or even worse—was there some sort of forgery involved? The question must be asked, because Velma was a major fraudster and serial forger.

Once we get past the matter of how it was that she became the beneficiary of his life insurance policy, we can't help but wonder about the manner of this guy's strange and sudden death. His official cause of death was listed as "accidental". It's said that he walked out into traffic and was hit by a truck in the middle of the night.

Velma was the chief architect of this story, claiming that he walked off, stayed gone, and the next thing she knew he had been flattened by oncoming traffic. That's fine—accidents *do* happen. But since countless souls perished because of Velma's supposed accidents—accidents that later proved to be intentional murder—we have to take a second look at all of this.

Could it be that Velma the Master Manipulator somehow caused this man's death. She might not have pushed him out into the road (then again, maybe she did!), but perhaps she just arranged for him to be in just the wrong place at just the wrong time. Maybe he was drunk and she intentionally directed him to cross a busy road in the hope that he would get flattened.

After it was all said and done, she was awarded with a check for $5,000. Which was a pretty good chunk of change back in the early 1970s. But as was typically the case, Velma and her drug habit made short work of this windfall. And by Christmas she was once again broke.

So broke in fact, that she gave her mother Lillian a decidedly bad Christmas surprise, by taking a loan out on her car. The car had been paid off years ago by Murphy, yet Velma found a way to circumvent her mother and take a loan out on the vehicle. Lillian was considerably confused just before New Year's, when she was getting letters in the mail demanding that she pay up.

She wouldn't have long to worry about even this frustration however, because Lillian herself wasn't long for this world. Just before the New Year rolled around, she suddenly became deathly ill. Velma alerted relatives that Lillian was throwing up blood and she was rushed to the hospital. Doctors couldn't figure out exactly what was wrong with her, but Lillian was rapidly deteriorating right before their eyes.

Ronnie was alerted to what had happened in the meantime and rushed to the hospital. By the time he arrived, Velma was pacing back and forth down a hall outside Lillian's hospital room, sobbing and crying. In between her sobs, she informed Ronnie that his Grandma Lillian was already dead.

As much as Ronnie wished to save his tears for his deceased grandmother, Velma once again made sure that all of the attention was on her, as she cried up a storm and demanded that all sympathy be sent in her direction.

Sure, it was her mother that had died—she had a right to be sad. Little did anyone know however, that Velma was the one who had killed her.

Sobering Realization

In the aftermath of her mother's death, Velma was still in no condition to stand on her own two feet. Both Pamela and Ronnie took turns allowing their mother to stay with them. Velma continued to take way too many pills however, and overdoses kept sending her to the hospital. The police in the meantime, had been given an arrest warrant because of bad checks that she had been forging.

Ronnie and Pamela were both at a loss. But it was Pamela who decided enough was enough, and determined to cut off all help. She figured that perhaps facing up to what she had done was the best medicine her mother could possibly receive at this point. So it was, when her mother begged and pleaded for help out of this latest jam, Pamela was determined to set her straight.

In no uncertain terms, Pamela told her, "You got into this. I tried to help you, and you wouldn't listen. Now you'll have to get out of it yourself." Ronnie wholeheartedly agreed, and after she was subsequently arrested, he refused to pay her bail. Her children had determined that perhaps jail was the best place for their mother at the moment. So it was, that Velma rang in the New Year of 1975 behind bars.

It wasn't until March 21st of that year, that Velma finally got to see a judge. Standing before the judge on that fateful day, with all of the pills finally out of her system, she was likely the most sober she had been in decades. She faced the music, and the judge handed down a heavy sentence. He demanded that she serve no less than six months in the North Carolina Correctional Center for Women, in Raleigh, North Carolina.

No less than half a year of her life would be spent in prison for the forgeries she had tried to pull off. Although Velma had managed to sober up at this point, she was soon complaining of acute withdrawal symptoms. Amazingly enough, the doctors at the prison actually prescribed her Valium, apparently just to get her through the day.

Her family likely thought that prison time would help her to face her addiction and sober up, little did they know that the prison doctors would continue to supply her while she was behind bars. And despite the judge's insistence on her serving six months, her time was ultimately cut in half, and she was out after just a few months served.

She was then back out on the streets by June 30th, 1976.

At first her family was hopeful that she had turned over a new leaf. For the first time in her life, Velma seemed to have taken some responsibility for her actions. She might not yet have been ready to admit that she was a mass murdering serial killer, but she did quietly concede that she had a major addiction problem and she reasoned that her addiction had caused her to "waste some of the best years of her life."

She also promised that she would try to keep off the drugs and do better. Many addicts have made this promise to hopeful loved ones. And like so many others, Velma's kids found that all they could do was hope and pray that this time *would be different*—that this time she *would* get better. Well—it was better for about a week, until Velma once again overdosed and ended up in the hospital.

For Ronnie and Pamela, it was as if their old nightmare had returned after a three-month hiatus. The three months that their mother was in jail, they didn't have to deal with her constant, life-draining issues. But now she was back in their life, and in less than a week, was back to causing the same old chaos and disturbances.

Even worse, soon it was discovered that she was back to her old tricks of forging checks. Demonstrating that she had learned absolutely nothing from her previous incarceration for forgery, this time around she had forged checks under the name of Pamela's husband Kirby. Needless to say, Kirby would have been none too pleased to find all of this out.

He had taken his mother-in-law under his own roof in an effort to help her, and this was how she repaid him? By forging checks under his name and stealing his money? A family intervention was in order. Ronnie confronted her over the issue, and Velma begged them to not take action and to give her another chance.

She insisted that she wouldn't be able to handle going back to prison, and cried and begged until Ronnie promised he would find a way to smooth things over. He convinced Pamela to pay off the checks before Kirby got wind of it.

Velma's probation officer in the meantime, had lined up a "halfway house" for Velma, located in Charlotte, North Carolina. Velma didn't like the idea of being in a structured, supervised program. She likely realized that her drug use would be strictly monitored and didn't want her substance abuse to be hampered.

She threw a fit and begged her adult children not to put her in the halfway home. They finally relented. She would continue to stay with Pamela. Velma in the meantime, had promised that she would straighten up her act. and even got a job. She found work as a caregiver for a local, elderly woman.

The job involved Velma living with the lady and taking care of her needs. The woman was facing steep mental decline however, and the job was fairly frustrating for Velma. She later claimed that it was so frustrating, that she had to medicate in order to cope with it. This, of course, is a cop-out, since there are plenty of folks who do plenty of frustrating jobs without having to make themselves high as a kite in the process.

It was in the first few months of 1976 in the meantime, that even this gig petered out when the woman she had been caring for was placed into a nursing home. The lady's sister however, who had been the principal employer for Velma, appreciated her work enough to refer her to another patient. She was directed to become the caregiver for a certain Montgomery Edwards.

The 94-year-old Montgomery Edwards was suffering from diabetes. Diabetes so severe that he had gone blind and lost his legs. The man couldn't get out of bed, and like an infant, had to have his every need cared for. It was his 84-year-old wife Dollie who was seeking the extra help to take care of her ailing husband. Dollie was not in the best health herself, but she was strong-willed, and certainly strongly opinionated as it pertained to the care of her husband.

For her efforts, Velma was given room and board as well as her allotted $75 paycheck. She would live with the Edwards, but their home was still within reach of Pamela, so Pam periodically checked in on her mother to see how she was getting along. Velma seemed to enjoy her job as tiring as it might have been. She especially enjoyed sitting and talking with Dollie during her downtime.

She also enjoyed conversing with the ailing Montgomery, during his few moments of clarity during the day. Velma also started going to a local Pentecostal church during this time. She didn't have her own transportation, but she was able to get there by way of a church bus that dutifully came to pick her up on Sundays as well as on Wednesdays.

The fact that she didn't have transportation however created problems when it came to her many doctor's appointments. This often meant her adult children were on duty to have to give her a ride. It was on March 11th, that it was Ronnie's turn to serve as chauffeur, and he dutifully picked up his mother to take her to yet another appointment. His wife Joanna who was eight months pregnant at the time, joined him for the ride.

The ride there was fine, and Velma's appointment was fine, but it was after Velma requested to drive the car back, that a major problem occurred. Ronnie despite his better judgment, let his mother get behind the wheel. Velma drove well enough at first, but when a car began to brake in front of her, she overreacted and slammed on the brakes. This caused her to lose control of the car.

The car careened into the middle of the road and they were hit by a Ryder truck. Ronnie got the worst of it in this exchange since his head was sent slamming into the windshield. He was covered in blood. Despite his injuries, it was Ronnie who pulled everyone else from the wreckage, making sure that everybody was OK.

Fortunately, Joanna was able to give birth to her and Ronnie's child Michael, the following month, without any problems. This shocking experience coupled with the new grandchild, seemed to convince Velma to try a little harder.

She continued to work her job and seemed to do well. She got along well with both Dollie and Montgomery, and soon she was getting on well with a third person—Stuart Taylor.

Mr. Taylor was Dollie's nephew. He had met Velma during different visits, and the two had apparently hit it off fairly well. Ronnie met him on one occasion and was surprised that his mother was so taken by the guy. Even more surprised when he learned that the man was married. He and his wife had been separated it was true—but their divorce was not yet final.

Nevertheless, Velma began seeing Stuart Taylor, going out on dates with him on a fairly regular basis. He would come right over to his Aunt Dollie's place where Velma was staying and pick her up. He was a shining point of happiness and fun during her work days, which were otherwise monotonous and boring.

It was with great disappointment that Velma learned that Stuart Taylor had patched things up with his wife and would have to stop seeing her. Velma acted as if she took the whole thing in her stride, but the work situation at Dollie's place rapidly went downhill after this. She got into increasingly heated arguments with Dollie over the care of Montgomery.

Dollie grew displeased with how Velma carried out her duties and more prone to criticize her. In many ways, the adversarial relationship that Velma developed with the older woman. was very similar to the one that she had formed with her mother Lillian. Even more startling, it would end with the same results, when just like Lillian, Dollie would turn up dead.

They Just Keep Dropping Like Flies

On January 29th, 1977, old man Montgomery died at 95 years old. With his death, Velma had lost her reason for employment. By all accounts she should have moved on, but Dollie apparently decided to let Velma stay for a while. Instead of taking care of Montgomery, she was now basically a maid, at the beck and call of Dollie.

The fact that Dollie could be a harsh taskmaster only increased Velma's resentment and animosity. She wouldn't have long to worry about it however, because a little over a month after her husband Montgomery died, Dollie too would perish. Dollie first became deathly ill on February 26th. She was throwing up and having terrible stomach pains. The next day she was taken to the hospital.

She was sent home, but didn't get better. That Tuesday she returned to the hospital and died in intensive care. Even though Velma played the part of a shocked and saddened former carer, it would later be learned that Dollie was likely poisoned by none other than Velma Barfield.

Killing Dollie in some sense, had Velma shooting herself in the foot. Because after the death of her latest elderly benefactor, Velma was out of a place to live. This meant that her adult children Ronnie and Pamela were once again on duty to figure out what her next living arrangements might be.

She stayed with them only a week however, before opportunity called. It was the pastor of Velma's church in fact, who called her up, to recommend her to a local elderly woman named Record Lee, who had broken her leg in a bad fall. She was 76 and her husband John Henry Lee was 80. Neither one had the full capacity to run the household, without a little help. Velma leapt at the opportunity.

At first things went well enough, Velma cooked, cleaned, and took care of all of the household chores. Things took a bad turn however, when Record Lee noticed that a check had been forged in her name. John Henry looked into it, and decided to call the police. It was shortly after he made this fateful call, that he began to get sick.

He was nauseated and having terrible stomach pains. He was taken to the hospital where his condition only got worse. He ultimately passed on June 4th of that year. Velma was very attentive to the family members in the aftermath, and they insisted that she stay on to help the recently widowed Record Lee. Little did they know the risk that they were exposing this poor old woman to.

For it was Velma and her penchant for sneaking poison into her charges' food and drinks which had been making them sick and killing them. These facts wouldn't come to light until later, but Velma had become quite proficient with the use of arsenic, a tasteless poison that is not easily traced upon cursory examination.

Fortunately for Record Lee and her family members, she proved to be one of the victims that got away. Because for whatever reason, after she survived the first round of arsenic poisoning that Velma had exposed her to—Velma let Record Lee off the hook. The old woman had become very sick, but recovered. For whatever reason, Velma decided to leave it at that. And after Record Lee got out of the hospital, Velma abruptly informed her family that she wouldn't be able to work for them any longer and was going to go her separate way.

Her next victim however, would not be so lucky. For it was after the aborted murder attempt on Record Lee, that Velma sunk her arsenic-dripping teeth into her old flame Stuart Taylor. Stuart had arrived on the scene just in time to tell Velma that his divorce from his previous, estranged wife, had been finalized.

By the time summer rolled around, the two were going everywhere together. They would even go on weekend-long trips. These trips involved shacking up in hotel rooms where they consummated their relationship. Velma was doing all of this on the side while regularly attending church services where such extramarital activity was strictly condemned.

It didn't bother Velma in the slightest however, since she was quite used to living in two different worlds. It wasn't hard for her to have her fun with Stuart on Saturday and then attend a church service on Sunday looking demure and devout, singing "Amen" with the choir. Velma in the meantime, had left the Lee home and rented out a trailer for herself.

She supposedly wanted to have more space and freedom to do as she wished with Stuart Taylor. Strangely enough however, it was after Velma was away from Record Lee, that Ms. Lee made a full recovery. Yet another stunning coincidence? Of course not. In hindsight, it would be realized that Lee's surge of good health was thanks to the absence of Velma and her arsenic.

Velma was moving on however, and in fact, shortly thereafter she would move right in with Stuart Taylor himself. But she had to put on her own strange and warped idea of a pressure campaign in order to do so. She actually scared the poor man into letting her move in, by staging an attack on herself. She had arranged for him pay her a visit, and had left her door unlocked.

Right before Stuart arrived however, she stripped down to her undies, put tape on her mouth, and tied herself up. This set the scene, so that Stuart would waltz right into her home to find her moaning and crying, restrained and prostrate on her bed. Stuart didn't know what to think of it, and Velma was so incoherent, he couldn't even begin to get any information out of her. Nevertheless, the poor bewildered fellow called the police.

The police managed to get her to calm down enough to give an account. But upon further questioning, the alleged crime did not make any sense. Velma claimed that someone came into her apartment and tied her up. Yet, when asked what happened next—Velma claimed the perpetrator simply left.

It didn't make sense to the average listener—nor to seasoned detectives either. Based on Velma's account, detectives couldn't fathom any kind of motive on the part of a hypothetical perpetrator. As suggestive as the pose of Velma tied up on her bed in her undergarments might have been, Velma insisted that she had not been sexually assaulted.

With the motive of a sex crime ruled out, the only other reason a criminal would barge into someone's house and restrain them would have been if they wanted to steal something. But this too was a dead end, because Velma insisted that nothing was stolen. So, what was the point of any of it? Unless it was a bizarre (and potentially prison-meriting) prank, it just didn't seem to add up.

…unless the whole thing was staged. And it was when detectives noticed the attention that Stuart Taylor showered on Velma, and saw how happy it made her—a possible motive began to take shape. It seemed likely that Velma faked the whole thing just to get attention and get Stuart to insist that she stay with him. They couldn't prove this is what happened, but they certainly had quite a hunch that this was indeed the case.

But if Velma thought that life with Stuart Taylor would be one big (unmarried) honeymoon, she was mistaken. They began to argue and have disagreements almost as soon as they started living together. It also wasn't long before Velma fell back on her old habit of forging checks. She forged two checks from Stuart's account. He found out about it later that month and was furious.

Velma left after a heated argument but soon returned. The marriage plans were off now, and Velma was once again staying with Pamela. It wasn't long before these arrangements broke down and Velma was trying her luck with Ronnie. Her son Ronnie, however, had finally had enough and told his mom as much.

For the first time ever, he told her that he couldn't deal with her antics any longer. He and his wife Joanna had their hands full with their own son, Michael, and they couldn't deal with the extra chaos that Velma caused them.

Instead of being at all apologetic for all of the damage and destruction she had dealt Ronnie through the years, his mother flew into a complete rage. She shouted and screamed that she just couldn't believe that her own son would "betray her" like this.

Before she stormed off, Ronnie recalled his mother giving him a look that was "unlike any [he'd] ever seen before." It was a look as if she could *kill.* Little did Ronnie know at the time, of course, that his angry, vengeful mother had already been *killed.*

The Final Victim

After having her son Ronnie's doors close to her, Velma bounced back and forth between Pamela's house and her boyfriend Stuart's home. Stuart's daughter Alice would later recall an incident in which Stuart brought Velma to her home. She had just had her baby boy, William, and Stuart wanted to show him off to Velma. The visit was pleasant enough, but later on, one episode in particular would stand out to Alice.

They were all looking through a photo album and Velma had made a point to ask to see Stuart Taylor's "dead picture." Alice knew exactly what she was talking about. It was an infamous photo that had been made as a joke at a previous family gathering. The photo was of Stuart lying on the coach, flat on his back with his arms folded against his chest, pretending he was dead.

It was just a gag, and the whole family thought it was pretty funny. It was only after her father ended up *truly dead* at the hands of Velma, that Alice would realize how shockingly frightening Velma's request was. It was shortly thereafter that her father Stuart's nightmare would begin. Shortly after this fateful visit with Alice, Stuart took Velma to see a well-known evangelist by the name of Rex Humbard.

Despite the fact that according to the Pentecostal standards of the day, Stuart and Velma were "living in sin," Stuart was eager to see the preacher. After drinking some beer and chowing down on a meal fixed by Velma, the two were off. Stuart only managed to sit through the first few minutes of the evangelist's preaching however, before he broke into a cold sweat.

And no, the cold sweat wasn't likely because of Rex Humbard's fire and brimstone preaching about how the apocalypse was near—Stuart was quite literally sick to his stomach. He was nauseous, and having terrible stomach pains. He excused himself, but insisted that Velma continue to sit and watch the service, while he went back to his truck.

Considering the fact that Velma and her penchant for poisoning folks, was the actual reason behind the man's illness, one can't help but wonder *how* she sat through a church service, in which audience members are asked to search their hearts, and ask forgiveness for any wrongdoing they had done in the past. Was Velma seeking absolution even as she was in the *process* of murder?

After getting back from the service however, Stuart Taylor only continued to get worse. He got so bad he was bedridden, with Velma attending to his every need. Little did he know that Velma was still slipping him poison at every opportunity too.

Soon Stuart was not only vomiting and having stomach pains, but his organs were failing him. He was rushed off to the hospital but shortly thereafter he perished from what seemed to be, to most onlookers, a sudden and mysterious illness.

Stuart Taylor was only 56 years old at the time, and he had previously enjoyed good and robust health. What had brought him down so quickly? How did this sudden turn for the worst take place? Velma was the only one with the answers to these questions, and she wasn't talking. It was only when the attending physician—Dr. Jordan—remarked that an autopsy should take place, that any real answers would be found.

It was the autopsy that would find the tell-tale signs of arsenic poisoning. The arsenic would be found in chunks of Stuart's liver. There was no reason that arsenic should be found in this grown man's liver—Stuart would not consume arsenic *willingly*. This man had clearly been poisoned. It was now just a question of who was it that did the poisoning? The most likely poisoner would be the one who had the closest proximity to the victim, which would place them in a position to administer poison to them.

A random stranger might be able to slip something in someone's drink on one occasion, but only an intimate associate could do it on a regular basis, as seemed to occur during Stuart's agonizing, slow and drawn-out death. Detectives assigned to the case soon became aware that the person who most easily fit this bill was Stuart's troubled girlfriend, Velma Barfield.

As much as Velma tried to present herself as a woman above reproach, police were already well aware that she was a drug addict with quite a criminal past. This was more than enough reason for police to view her as a suspect. And the deeper they dug into her background, the more disturbing things they found. They discovered that Velma had been married more than once, and had a string of boyfriends in between.

But most alarming, many of those close to Velma had *died* in sudden, distressing fashions. No one ever said her first husband, Thomas, was poisoned, but his death was sudden and strange all the same. He was found dead smoking a cigarette. Police wrote it off as an accident, but how could anyone know for sure? Velma's boyfriend Al Smith was yet another poor soul who perished from a sudden, inexplicable accident. His death brought with it a payout since Velma had somehow become the beneficiary of his life insurance policy.

Then there was the old man Jennings, her second husband, who died of a sudden onslaught of illness. This death actually matched the death of Stuart Taylor quite closely. For both of them seemed to experience acute gastrointestinal problems that had them throwing up with severe stomach pains, which ultimately led to their deaths. But beyond her love life, it was also discovered that others who just so happened to be in close proximity to Velma were likewise dropping like flies.

It was found that her own mother died under similarly strange circumstances, so had her father, and so had an elderly man she had once watched. The elderly man's wife also perished in this sudden manner.

Another man she cared for died the same way, and his wife very nearly succumbed to the same fate. There has to come a point when so many strange coincidences of death haunting one woman can no longer be considered coincidences.

The detectives immediately understood that Velma was likely behind most—if not all—of these deaths. This led the detectives to swoop down and question her. They wanted to put her on her heels so that they could rattle her, and get her to speak off the cuff. They figured that with any luck, they might even be able to coax a confession out of her.

They were going to do so by trying to shock the truth out of her. They wanted to get her in a corner and basically tell her, point blank, that they not only know that Stuart was poisoned, but they know that she did it. Of course, besides a strong hunch, they didn't really have proof yet that Velma was the culprit.

Nevertheless, it was this standard shock tactic employed in the interrogation room that the police hoped would get Velma to fess up to what she had done. They weren't quite prepared for Velma's antics however; she was ready to immediately do a psychological jujitsu move on the cops and turn herself into the victim—and turn them into unfair aggressors.

As soon as she realized she was being accused of poisoning Stuart she burst into tears and claimed that far from killing him, she loved him and was doing everything she could to help him. The police of course weren't going to be that easily dissuaded. Because no matter what Velma said, they still had a corpse full of arsenic. As such, the detectives naturally wanted to know, if she didn't give Stuart the arsenic, how did it get into his system?

Velma Barfield, for all of her bluff and bluster, couldn't readily spin this glaring detail; all she could do was shrug and say that she didn't know. The police then asked her if perhaps she would take a lie detector test to prove that she had no knowledge of the events that led up to Stuart Taylor's death. Being the narcissist that she was, she readily agreed.

Velma seemed pretty smug in her belief that she could trick even a lie detector test. But it was when one of the detectives mentioned that they were looking into a whole string of similar deaths that went all the way back to Velma's mother, that she finally had some pause. A Sheriff's Deputy, whose name comes down to us as "Alf Parnell" was at the scene, and later recalled the "sharp look" Velma gave, before turning away, indicating that they had indeed struck a chord with her.

They had caused the wheels of her mind to spin, but were they spinning towards confession, or simply coming up with more excuses? The detectives, in the meantime, informed Stuart Taylor's daughter Alice of their suspicions, and she was understandably livid. The fact that Velma might have done something so heinous, was like flipping a switch that changed Alice's whole world.

This revelation made Alice realize that the whole time she thought that Velma was selflessly helping her "sick and ailing" father, she was actually poisoning him. She wasn't helping him get better—on the contrary, she was actively making him get worse. She may not have put a gun to his head, but she had put Alice's dad through several days of agony, by slowly poisoning him until his organs shut down.

Her father's death was a terrible and tortuous one. It would have been much more merciful if Velma had ended him with a bullet, rather than the slow terrible death she inflicted on Stuart Taylor by way of arsenic poisoning. He lingered on for several days in absolute agony before his body finally gave out.

Arsenic is commonly used in rat poison, this too was insulting to Stuart Taylor and his family, since it was as if Velma thought so little of this man, that she put him down like he was nothing more than a rat. Playing the role of exterminator, she extinguished his life as easily as one would common vermin.

To learn all of these startling details, Alice was beyond infuriated, but it wouldn't be long before Velma would come calling, to try and give *her side of the story.* It was shortly after Alice had been tipped off by police, that Velma rang her up and rattled off a long angry tirade about how the police dared to suspect her of wrongdoing. She claimed that the police must be involved in an active cover up, attempting to hide what had *really happened to Stuart.*

Alice had been previously advised to act as if she were still friends with Velma and to behave as if she didn't suspect Velma of killing her father. This was done so that Velma would keep her guard down, and enhance the possibility that she might unintentionally incriminate herself in conversation. Detectives on the case in the meantime, came across a series of checks that were fraudulently written in Stuart's name.

One of them was written the very day that Stuart Taylor first got sick and was cashed the day before he actually died. Detectives on the case believed that this was a clear indication for motive. Velma had already been caught forging checks in the past, and she didn't want Stuart to turn her in when he inevitably found out, so she simply killed him instead. This was more than enough to charge her with murder.

It was then that March that Velma was officially brought up on murder charges. She attended a hearing on March 14th, 1978, in which she was appointed a public defender, since she couldn't afford to hire an attorney. Her public attorney was a guy by the name of Bob Jacobson.

It was through her attorney Bob that Velma finally gave—at least a partial—confession. She admitted to him that it was true that she had poisoned Stuart, and that she had also killed others. She hadn't admitted the full number that she had killed, which would come to grow over time. She did admit however, that Stuart was her final victim, among several others whom she had poisoned.

Trial and Sentencing

After her arrest, it was determined that Velma had not killed one—but several people. Of particular interest were John Henry Lee, Dollie Edwards, and Velma's own mother Lillian Bullard. These bodies were exhumed for posthumous autopsy purposes. Ronnie was disturbed to hear of the possibility that his mother had done all of this, and so too was Pamela.

Pamela in particular, was horrified that Velma could have done something to her sweet grandmother Lillian. As much as Velma hated the woman, Pamela loved her dearly. But even more alarming was a matter that Pamela's husband, Kirby, subsequently raised in regard to an evening that they were both terribly ill. Pamela had almost forgotten about the episode, but the memory came rushing back to her as a consequence of all of the things being brought up for the trial.

It had occurred during one of the many stints of Velma crashing at their home, and after a particularly terrible argument with her. Velma had demanded the use of their car and Pamela had politely declined. She knew that her mom was going to take it to go and get drugs, and she was worried for her safety. She also didn't want her accident-prone mother to wreck another car.

Pamela declined, and Velma stormed off in a rage. It was later that night that both Pamela and Kirby began throwing up and having terrible stomach pains. They wondered if it was something they ate. As it turns out, it was. They had eaten some food that Velma had managed to put some poison in.

That evening Kirby had sworn that the tea that Velma had given them after the dinner before they got sick "tasted a little funny." At the time, they didn't think much of it. But now that Velma was on trial for poisoning multiple people, it seemed pretty clear to Pamela that her own mother had tried to kill her. And for what? Because her daughter wouldn't let her mother drive her car?

This was a woman who clearly had no remorse for any of her actions. It was all about her. She was more than willing to kill the very people who were helping her—her own family—for no better reason than her own sheer spitefulness. As shockingly dreadful as all of this was, the only thing that Pamela and Ronnie could cling to was the good memories of their mother when they were small children.

Back then she was kind, loving, and nurturing. The woman who had read children's stories to them and spent just about every waking moment seeing to their needs, seemed like a completely different character than the woman that had emerged in later years. Pamela and Ronnie had concluded that the woman that killed all those people *was not the mother they knew.*

Instead, her drug-addled mind had transformed her into a warped caricature of what she once was. Predictably enough, it all sounded good enough to Velma and played right into her criminal defense. For when she faced her first indictment of first-degree murder for Stuart Taylor, she pled "not guilty by reason of insanity." In other words, Velma agreed that she had somehow been warped and changed over time, changed into something that was not quite normal, not quite sane.

So she pled not guilty by reason of insanity, arguing that she essentially wasn't in her right mind at the time of the murders. The insanity plea has left many cynical over the years, due to the way that it's often been seen as an excuse for killers to get away with murder. One could actually argue that just about *anyone* who would intentionally kill someone else, could qualify as insane.

Most of us "normal people" after all, don't go around killing folks. Having said that, in the broadest of terms, if the insanity plea was invoked often enough, it would be hard to find any killer guilty of anything. All a murderer would have to do was argue that they were insane at the time of the incident, and they would get off. It's due to this sort of complexity that it must be extensively argued when and where one should draw the line as it pertains to this defense.

Velma's attorney, Bob Johnson, made the plea on her behalf, and it was then up to the courts to decide what to make of it all. Velma's trial began on November 27th, 1978. Despite all she had done to them, many of Velma's family members were there to show their support for their mother turned killer—Velma Barfield.

Even though she had admitted to killing four people at this point, she was actually only on trial for the murder of Stuart Taylor. This is often done in serial murder cases, since it only takes one conviction of murder to put a killer away for life or have them handed a death sentence. This was the strategy at Velma's trial, with prosecutors focusing on Stuart Taylor's case, since it was the most recent and likely the easiest to convict Velma Barfield on. And if this failed, the prosecution planned to open up the other murder cases as a last resort.

The first step was assembling the jury, which was overseen by an overzealous prosecutor intent upon getting a jury pool favorable to the death penalty. One juror in fact was dismissed after they point blank stated that they didn't believe in capital punishment.

Eventually however, the prosecution assembled a jury which was deemed to be "death-qualified." In other words, a jury in which all of the jurors supported the concept of the death penalty, and wouldn't hesitate to find a suspect guilty, even if it meant that it would result in a death sentence. It was once the jury was formed that the trial began in earnest.

The biggest moment of the trial's first phase was when the prosecution's witnesses were called to the stand. First up was Stuart Taylor's son, Billy Taylor. Billy was questioned about how his father appeared to him when he visited him at the hospital. Billy described a dreadful sight in which his father was in constant pain, and even worse, couldn't seem to sit still.

He kept sitting up, only to quickly lie down and then sit up again. It was as if his stomach were being eaten up by acid, and he couldn't help but constantly move and react to it. For someone who had ingested a deadly poison, this is precisely the physical reaction that one might expect. Just like a rat which had ingested rat poison and was found writhing around in a rat trap—Velma's victims met a similar fate.

Next up on the witness stand was an ER doctor named Leland Jones. Mr. Jones was on the scene when Stuart Taylor had been rushed to the emergency room, and had seen first-hand, this incredibly distressed patient. Jones seconded Billy's description, stating that Stuart had been making "writhing movements." The most damning testimony however likely came from a paramedic by the name of John McPherson who was present during some of Stuart's final most tortuous moments.

McPherson concurred with Billy Taylor and Leland Jones that Stuart seemed unable to sit still, as if something was eating him up inside forcing him to move back and forth. McPherson also noted that Stuart was breathing very rapidly, and that his skin had turned to a strange, grey sheen. Most startling was the sound effects that McPherson described.

He stated that Stuart was moaning and groaning continually, but the worst came when he suddenly threw back his head and gave a "bloodcurdling scream." Seeing an opportunity to demonstrate to the jurors just how terrible the scene really was, the prosecutor asked the witness if he could imitate the sound that he heard. The witness readily obliged.

To the shock of everyone in the courtroom, McPherson threw back his head and screamed, a horrible, painful sounding scream. It was certainly something that no one would forget—especially the jurors who were tasked with determining Velma Barfield's fate. It was after this dreadful description of Stuart Taylor's last moments on Earth, that his daughter Alice took the stand.

She testified how her dad had been in great health just days prior to his sudden illness, and how he and Velma had both visited her, seemingly in a good mood. It was not long after this fateful visit that Velma called up Alice out of the blue to report that Stuart Taylor wasn't feeling well. She asked Alice if maybe she should give him an aspirin.

Considering the fact that Velma had no qualms with administering poisonous arsenic to the girl's father, the fact that she would ask about aspirin, was just more of her callous games. It was an entirely false façade for her to pretend she really cared what Alice thought about a little dose of aspirin, since she obviously never bothered to mention the fact that she had already given him a large dose of arsenic!

Alice told her she thought aspirin would be fine. Alice then called back a short time after that and reported that Stuart was better and she had made him his favorite meal—oyster stew. This was a sticking point for the prosecution since they knew that Velma poisoned folks through food and drink. Alice testified that Velma had informed her that Stuart ate the stew.

It was apparently after he ate this fateful stew that he became deathly ill. Alice reported that she would only briefly see her father in a hospital room before he had perished. The next witness for the prosecution was the pathologist who had performed the autopsy, Bob Andrews. Mr. Andrews was the one who had discovered the arsenic that had worked its way into Stuart Taylor's vital organs.

As the poison worked its way into his tissue, the terrible sensation that Stuart felt caused him to writhe in agony. His body was telling him something was wrong—lethally wrong—but he didn't know what to do except, writhe, shake, and scream. Arsenic is hard for anyone to trace, and even an expert pathologist might miss it during a cursory examination.

It was the expertise of pathologist Bob Andrews that found traces of arsenic had worked their way deep into the man's vital organs. It was his liver especially that bore the brunt of the arsenic. The liver naturally seeks to absorb and rid the body of potential toxins. It's for this reason that alcoholics often end up with an overburdened liver, due to all of the liver's efforts to absorb alcohol. But absorbing vodka and whiskey, as taxing as it might be, can be done—absorbing arsenic however is another story.

Even the strongest liver would not be able to withstand a heavy dose of arsenic for very long. In later days as the trial progressed, more testimony from other witnesses would follow. In particular there was testimony from the Lee family. Recorder Lee was almost killed by Velma but survived, her husband John Henry however, was not quite as fortunate.

To be certain, Velma was only actually standing trial for the murder of Stuart Taylor, but even so, the prosecution sought to demonstrate the impact that Velma had on so many others. As such, Margie Lee Pittman took the stand to testify about how her father—John Henry—spent his last few moments in utter agony. He was groaning, moaning and screaming as sweat dripped from his heavily perspiring face.

Margie Lee Pittman described how she actually wiped the sweat free from his face, even while the old man moaned. According to Margie Lee, his agony was so great, he just couldn't keep still. He was moving all over the bed. The agony that this man suffered was indeed very similar to how a rat reacts when they are given rat poison.

Arsenic of course, is the number one ingredient in rat poison, so such things do indeed make sense. Margie went on to narrate how her father died in that hospital, and how she and her family sat through the funeral. She described how Velma presented herself as a caring, compassionate person who just wanted to help, but this of course, was most certainly *not* the case.

The next witness of note, was a certain Dr. Joe Alexander. Dr. Joe Alexander was a local physician based out of Lumberton, who had over 25 years of experience at the time. He was also quite familiar with arsenic and what it could do to someone who had unwittingly ingested it. Most of the instances of arsenic poisoning of course, are not murderous, but rather some sort of accidental ingestion.

There are indeed cases of folks accidentally ingesting rat poison for example, by way of a series of unfortunate mishaps. Just imagine someone haphazardly putting rat poison on the top shelf of the pantry, only for some of it to fall into the cookie jar on the shelf down below! Such things might sound pretty ridiculous—but they have happened, and have led to some pretty terrible results.

These were likely the sorts of cases that Dr. Alexander was most likely familiar with. Accidental poisoning, and not murder. But either way, the results were pretty much the same. The only element missing with accidental poisoning is the deception which is so keenly present in a case of murder by poisoning.

For if someone is accidentally poisoned as in the previous hypothetical situation described, it wouldn't take much to figure out what had caused the illness. In this scenario, someone accidentally eats a cookie touched by rat poison and gets terribly sick.

Shortly thereafter, someone else (perhaps a relative) opens up the pantry and is shocked to find that a box of rat poison on the top shelf of the pantry had opened, and some of the powder had fallen into the cookie jar. The startled relative then informs the attending physicians and immediate action is taken to counteract the poison.

In this scenario, there is a good chance that the patient will survive. But in the case of murder by way of arsenic poisoning, it is precisely the willful deception of the person doing the poisoning, which prevents any of these life-saving actions from happening. The poisoning in such a case is no accident, it's a deliberate act that the person who administered the poison is fully aware of.

And rather than inform the doctors of what is ailing the subject, the killer purposefully deceives and perhaps even leads attending physicians away from the cause of poison. The poisoner knows full well the cause of the sickness, and purposefully leads doctors and nurses astray.

In such a scenario, one could imagine someone like Velma, dumbly declaring, "Oh! I don't know what's wrong with him! He just had oyster stew and got sick!"

It's this wall of deception put up by the perpetrator that makes purposeful poisoning so much more deadly than accidental poisoning. For the unfortunate victim of murder by poisoning has everything against them as it pertains to any real *solution* to their dilemma; whereas the accidental poisoning victim has folks actively trying to correct and solve the problem.

It was Dr. Alexander who highlighted this dilemma of deception most keenly when he stated, "His recovery from the illness in April was good, and the diagnosis of gastroenteritis seemed perfectly logical. No one came forward with a suspicion that poisoning might have occurred."

Dr. Alexander was referring to the fact that Stuart Taylor had previously taken ill, when Velma had first poisoned him, and he had gone to a doctor. He seemed to get better (after getting away from Velma and her poison) and he was subsequently diagnosed with gastroenteritis. This seemed logical enough to the good doctor since no one had mentioned that there might be any possibility of poisoning having taken place.

Velma, of course, wouldn't have mentioned poison. So unfortunately for poor Stuart, there was no attempt to find the real cause of his ailment, since it was being buried under Velma's own willful, active, deception. All it would have taken was one word from Velma—and attending physicians could have administered an anti-arsenic agent known as BAL (British anti-lewisite) which can immediately counteract arsenic.

This could have saved Stuart's life. But of course, Velma didn't want that. She intended for Stuart Taylor to die. She did not say one word to save the man. She willfully allowed him to perish. This alone is a clear sign of premeditated murder in the first degree.

It was explosive testimony such as this, from family members and physicians alike, that would ultimately erode Velma's defense teams' efforts to get her off the hook for the death penalty.

It was Just an Accident

After endless rounds of damning testimony from both professional physicians, and anguished family members of victims, Velma's defense team felt that the only option they had left was to have Velma take the stand herself, to tell her side of the story. This was a huge gamble, basically a roll of the dice in the courtroom.

But at this point, it seemed that it might be the *only* chance that they might have left to sway the jury. Velma had been portrayed as a terrible monster of a human being, and now it was up to her to try and present her case.

Ironically, it was her penchant for manipulation, and deceptively portraying herself in a better light which were the main traits of her toxic personality. And yet, her defense team was now basically asking her to bring out these toxic tools in an attempt to actively manipulate the jury into liking her well enough to avoid the death penalty.

Velma's testimony was very hard to believe however, because it was so entirely at odds with what seemed to be pure and simple facts, as laid out by the prosecution. Because despite the mountain of damning evidence against her, Velma got up there and basically stated that she never wanted to kill anyone.

She stated that she only wanted to make folks sick. As odd as all of that is—as if making people sick was better than killing them—she stuck to this script. In a very cynical sort of way though, the logic of it does make *some* sense. Because Velma knew that her defense team were trying to lessen the charge from premeditated first-degree murder, to a lower one, that would not carry as heavy a penalty.

If she could convince the jurors that she was only trying to make folks sick and that she had *accidentally* killed several people, that takes away the premeditation. It would be a stretch to say that she had committed manslaughter after poisoning multiple people, but the threshold would indeed go down if it could be proven that she never really intended to kill anyone. If they were lucky, she could perhaps have it dropped from first-degree murder to second-degree murder.

No matter how much Velma tried to stick to this version of events however, upon cross examination it just didn't hold water. It was after this defense collapsed, that her defense team reverted back to using Velma's own tortured mind as her best defense.

They attempted to portray her mind as being so badly affected from habitual drug use, that she no longer really knew what it was that she was doing.

She testified to as much, claiming that before that fateful revival service she and Stuart Taylor had attended, she had put poison in Stuart's beer, just because she wanted to "make him sick." She supposedly wanted to make him sick, after he threatened to call the police on her over the check she had forged in his name. The reasoning behind such a thing, unless it was pure and simple spite, is hard to fathom.

Did she think that if she made him sick enough, he would be so bogged down recovering from an illness that he would forget that she had forged the check? This seems to have been the argument that was made—that she made him sick as a distraction—but things had simply gone too far when he actually *died* from being poisoned. But even if one could entertain such a notion, the clear deception that she demonstrated to everyone involved, was hard for them to explain.

Even when Velma's own attorney Jacobson questioned her as to why she didn't tell hospital staff of the acute poisoning that Stuart Taylor was suffering from—her answer was lackluster at best, and damning at worst. Her answer was simply that she, "didn't want to get in trouble." In other words, she was willfully deceiving everyone to save her own skin.

If Velma was that *out of her mind*, how was she capable of going to such elaborate (one might even say, clever) lengths to hide her crimes? She wouldn't have been able to—and of course, that fact stuck in the mind of the jurors who would ultimately decide her fate. Even worse however, was the cross examination by the prosecution. Because rather than presenting herself as the sympathetic elderly lady that her defense team had hoped, she came across as unapologetically angry, even scornful of those who questioned her.

She got into several sparring matches with the prosecutor in which she seemingly denied already proven facts of the case, and became angry at the most basic of questions, when they didn't fit her narrative. In other words, she basically showed her true colors as a belligerent manipulator, who liked to try and control events with her own deceptive machinations.

Rather than appearing as a meek and mild old lady, she appeared deceptive, combative, and downright dangerous. She appeared as someone who you wouldn't want to make angry—especially if she was about to handle your food! One can only imagine the discussions that went on between jurors during their lunch break.

Perhaps in lighter moments they even cracked jokes about it. Dark humor is often the greatest form of relief during tense trials such as this. Just imagine a juror during down time, grimacing after taking a bite out of a sandwich and muttering, "Dang! My food tastes funny! Tell the bailiff to make sure that Velma Barfield doesn't have access to my lunch box!"

But even if they could force themselves to laugh about it, if they were honest with themselves, any one of those jurors could clearly see how this mean, bitter, and spiteful woman could kill any one of them at the drop of the hat, with little care or remorse. It could have just as easily been them. In all seriousness, Velma Barfield was a clear and present danger to society.

Velma's own son Ronnie, had to admit his mother presented herself in the worst possible light while on the witness stand. Or as he later reflected, "She seemed to have no remorse about what she had done. I saw a mean person, a callous person who didn't seem to care what happened."

It was folks like Velma Barfield for whom the death penalty was designed. For unrepentant, murderous monsters who are a clear threat to society. The death penalty is not so much a punishment as it is a tool of removal—to remove clear and present threats from the civilized world.

Society is made up of rules that bind us all together; one of those rules of course being that we don't randomly kill people out of sheer spite. Velma however, had broken this sacred social compact, and seemed ready to continue poisoning anyone who so much as made her upset. Such a person cannot remain in society.

Lest she poison fellow inmates and prison staff, she was deemed too dangerous to even stay alive in prison. A life sentence wasn't even an option. It was indeed the death penalty that this jury would prescribe.

The Jury Has Decided

It didn't take long for the jury to finish deliberations and decide Velma Barfield's ultimate fate. She was found guilty of murder in the first degree, and for her crimes she was given the death penalty. She was then shuffled off to Central Prison, located in Raleigh, North Carolina, where she would sit on death row.

She remained on death row over the next few years, where she would be, by all accounts, a model inmate. One can surely question her sincerity, since she was known to be an extremely duplicitous character for much of her life, but Velma claimed to have undergone a jailhouse conversion. She professed to have become an ardent Christian, and spent her days witnessing the gospel to fellow inmates.

She was so prolific in her efforts, that she even managed to get a good word from the televangelist giant of the time—*Billy Graham.* Her efforts even led to folks like Graham to seek to have her death sentence commuted. She seemed reformed enough now, and she was doing God's work behind bars. Couldn't she simply be given a life sentence instead?

That seemed to be the argument that many well-meaning folks made. The more cynical among us however, might wonder if Velma's last-minute stab at becoming a Christian evangelist behind bars, just might have been yet another attempt to avoid the death penalty. Because when these efforts ultimately fell flat, she seemed to have tried an entirely different tactic.

Instead of seeking commutation on the grounds of being an exemplary example to her fellow inmates. She began to get prison psychiatrists to vouch that she was indeed insane. She even began to speak in the voices of multiple personalities, such as a personality she called "Billy."

Maybe Barfield realized that if she could convince folks that she wasn't the one who killed all those people (or at least that she wasn't in the driver's seat of her own mind) and that it was her other personality, Billy, who did it—maybe they would let her go?

Such tactics did not work on the judge however, who famously remarked that he didn't care whether it was Velma or her personality, Billy, who was guilty. One of them did it, and by carrying out Velma's execution he could get rid of them both. Seeing that this latest attempt wouldn't work, Velma seemed to finally accept her fate.

Her day of execution arrived on November 2nd, 1984. Many witnesses had gathered to see her off, including Anne Graham Lotz, the daughter of the aforementioned, sympathetic evangelist, Billy Graham. After a last meal which consisted of a can of Coca-Cola and a bag of cheez doodles, Velma Barfield was given a dose of her own medicine.

With a terrible and sickening irony, she was executed by way of lethal injection. It might not have been arsenic that was pumped into her veins, but she was injected with a lethal brew of chemicals all the same. In short order, the state had ended the unmitigated terror that had been her life.

Further Readings

Now that we have brought this book to its conclusion, let's take a moment to reflect on some of the reading and reference materials that helped bring this text about. Feel free to browse through this listing on your own.

Death Sentence: The True Story of Velma Barfield's Life, Crimes, and Execution. Bledsoe, Jerry
This book provides a pretty extensive account of Velma's life and her later crimes. It's a good reference, but it relies heavily on Velma's own testimony. Having that said, many of her past recollections—especially of her childhood—should be taken with a grain of salt. Even after killing multiple people, Velma typically tried to paint herself as the victim, and most of her early accounts as presented in Jerry Bledsoe's book, tend to express themselves in this fashion.

www.Dailymail.com
The Daily Mail has many articles on Velma that shed light on her crimes, trial, and execution.

Printed in Dunstable, United Kingdom